Pythagoras' Prison

Hank Youngman

2023

The following text is an informal essay. Parts have been fictionalized in varying degrees, for various purposes. The text is meant as literary entertainment only. The author bears no responsibility for any further inferences on the part of the reader. Citations and paraphrased text by other authors have been credited according to the MLA citation guidelines.

List of Contents

<u>Introduction</u>

Pythagoras' Prison should function in isolation, though the intent in its creation is to act as a piece of introductory writing to the text I had originally set out to write, titled *On Human Misunderstanding*. It is meant to address a problem that, unless addressed beforehand, puts the entire operation in jeopardy, for the capos the guards and the wardens (provided it ever reaches the latter), which metaphorical range I cover later in this essay, will be quick to call out a flaw in my reasoning that they have preemptively painted on canvas and called it proof of the crime: I write in ignorance of the mathematical reality of the subject, namely I write in ignorance of the correlation between a certain set of numbers and of numbered things that, though never subjects of numeric concern, nonetheless show a correlation that, even if not quite a correlation as much as a wishful coincidence, accounts for a dynamic between the system and the effect, such that, some would argue, to disagree with it is to live in ignorance of a coincidence too wishful not be the unambiguous cause.

At some indeterminate point in the not-too-distant past, the world of the humanities became usurped by something akin to dogmatism in regards to statistical proof. I do not mean that it *has come to cooperate with*, but rather that it *has been almost thoroughly conquered, colonized, and assimilated; and whatever is left is forced to collaborate with the tyrant.* I have no problem with the former. There certainly is room in the humanities for numbers, but numbers (or the people who revere them) have endeavored to claim intellectual territory that has in no sane epoch been subjected to mathematics. Indeed, economics is inseparable from math, but economic ethics are quite foreign to cold calculation. To argue otherwise and then use cold calculation to prove it makes for an argument too circular for its claim to reason. Art has nothing to do with math either. And yet, as I am writing this, the artists who liken themselves to the poets of yesteryear treat what should be their gift as no more than business, the kind that throttles quality in the name of profit, and spits in the faces of its patrons[1] if a statistical model predicts a possible diminishment of net income should promises be kept. Things are becoming ever bleaker as even honest artists are being cast to the side by a jumble of mathematical functions some proclaim constitute an intelligence while forgetting the disclaimer that it is by definition not.[2] The social scientist finds himself in a similar hell: whatever theory he might try to forward will be immediately put down by statistics and models that he has no way of disputing. This is not so because the facts are too good to dispute, but because there is nothing to be disputed. Statistical models are as reliable as fortunetellers. Speaking of, presenting in settings that may well hold the aesthetic successors of crystal balls and tarot cards, boasting of preternatural abilities to predict, and, for extra coin, to turn prediction into the power to influence, the kooks of modernity, one could argue, have adopted (and then readapted) the craft of the kooks of pre-modernity. It is superstition reimagined. No longer fooled by simple things like black cats and salt circles, the modern man is fooled by complex things like graphs and tables and charts. This air of mystery deters the ignorant and subjugates the naïve. But hey, *if the numbers say it, then so it must be* – just as long as we ignore the fact that the numbers can say whatever we want them to say, lest the first clause in italics acquires its true form.

Above are just a few general examples out of a multitude of problems resulting from the advancement of numbers before thought, but I should stress that my essay is not exclusively about the fall of academia to numeric authority. The more pressing issue is that the people among whom I presently walk have also been beguiled by the trend. This should worry us more than pretentious elites. It is the point at which an idea becomes integrated in the minds of the majority that it begins to have a truly negative impact – from the slavery of the previous era to the eugenics of the

---

[1] In the modern case loyal customers;
[2] I cover this in greater detail in the third essay.

previous century, to the unacknowledged slavery of this era and the emergent eugenics of the 21st century: evil is actualized as destruction only after it has been made manifest among the masses.

So I write *Pythagoras' Prison* first as a description of our intellectual incarceration, in case there are people who still mistake the prison for a fortress, and then as a meditation on how it happened, why it should not have happened, and, when thus considered, how we might leave it. It is only in this light that the essays that follow will have a chance to stand up to the dogma which opposition is the goal of their creation. I will employ a mostly indirect mode of expression, partly because it is how I have grown accustomed to writing whenever I write for fun, and partly because I seem to have developed a sense of pleasure at being misinterpreted by the intellectual capos guards and wardens, which happens so frequently that it just about proves my point: we are not dealing with a superior wizard – we are dealing with the hack of Oz.

So if I am to write anything else in the future, in particular, if I am to write about meaning, I must first get rid of the lowest possible objector to the sense I intend to discuss: the objector to sense and meaning altogether – the objector to anything that cannot be measured, the all too frequent argument that, if it cannot be counted, then it must not count.

Unless the reader is part of the prison staff, I believe they will find the text that follows a rather simple affair, and I hope they enjoy its wording. Conversely, if my book has fallen in the hands of a warden, then I wish him better pleasure in graphs and charts – and, heaven willing, perhaps a kind of pleasure that yet might fit on a table, and a table which, should the fates allow it, will by its rows and columns prove it a satisfaction that must be encouraged and spread among mankind, for it is in its impeccable benignity not to have cost the world its concept of morality that the replacement of meaning with math becomes validated as the optimal way to understand reality: a statistic is not a tragedy.

Part 1. Blocking

What is a Man?

What has he got? If not an income of a static value (adjusted for inflation), a definite mass, and three times as many feet as the average person, then he is not! If my reader has got the reference, they should be able to see the initial manifestation of the issue.

We hear in everyday speech that *a man is not a man* lest he can be said to comply to standards regarding such qualities as can be objectively presented in numbers, namely his relation to other men's measures in these same categories in a favorable ratio. These are such common expressions, that they even slip past conservative groups that take pride in their equivocation of sex and gender:[3] a man is a man as long as he is an adult human male – provided he also stands six feet tall, weighs around 190 pounds, owns a certain set of possessions, and earns a definite income! The conservative reader who uses these expressions might object: *We do not mean to say that a lack of these qualities makes one not-a-man; we merely mean to say that a man who stops short of these qualities is not a good man, i.e. he is a man of low quality!* My point still stands: in the minds of many, the value of man is determined not by his manhood, but by a tape-measure, a scale, and a bank account.

Just as the fact of labor is determined not by labor (or even quality) but by the money earned or the hours clocked in: four hours of intense labor is only half a job; eight hours of ineffective work is as real as it gets – however, two hours' worth of a CEO's input is considered working smart, whereas a year of writing a book that won't sell is considered a lazy indulgence. A schoolteacher who does not make a lot of money is said to be expendable, and a marketing-data-analyst with a six figure income is considered a productive member of society. It goes beyond economy. A man is regarded as sexually competent not

---

[3] Don't worry: this is not the argument you think it is.

on the quality of the women he likes, nor on his ability to turn down a woman he does not intend to make his long-term partner, but on the quantity of women with whom he has slept. A musician is successful not if he writes quality music, but if he fills out stadiums. The hungry artist is considered a poor artist because he is a poor man. An attempt to specify all the particular fields afflicted by such means of evaluation would be unnecessary for the scope of my argument, as its apparent universality stems from the fact of its generality. Is it not the case that *you are the only one who does this* is implied insanity and *the whole world does it* is an idiom of validation?

Therefore, having served their purpose, I will here pause with the examples, and proceed to draw attention to their absurdity. A man's value does not come from any measurable metric. Historically, great men have come in all shapes and sizes, and their success as men has rarely been tied to their ability to make money. I do not suppose Alexander the Great was regarded as great for his stature, nor do I think that Shakespeare is appreciated as one of the geniuses of entrepreneurship (rich though he was). Sound sexuality is a matter first of temperance, and then of standard.[4] And the association of art with fame has only led to the inhibition of quality art. As the reader has almost certainly noticed by now, our contemporary understanding of quality is but a numerical fallacy: it has no claim on reality proper; its sole claim is on reality measured.

I do not suppose it is at all controversial to say that manhood is determined by such qualities as are conceptually accessible to us all (courage, temperance, rationality, love, passion), and the same applies to labor and success and qualities too many in number to list here. All of these traits have been, out of time, glorified in masculine archetypes, and, within recorded time, confirmed in the annals of history. One needs no more metrics for masculinity than the myth of Hercules, nor does one need any more warnings

---

[4] The opposites are a weakness of character and a lack of self-respect (respectively).

against unbridled masculinity than this same myth, which, compared to stories with similar themes, will draw a picture of masculinity that no brute number, notwithstanding units of measure, can ever hope to achieve, for meaning is not a question of statistics, but of semantics (coded in words, not numerals).[5] If the concept of success is analyzed in this way, one might notice that it is conceptually synonymous with *being* (Chesterton, "Fallacy of Success") and thus realize the modern perversion in its narrowing equivocation with *being a wealthy man.* At last, in assessing sexuality, the concept of *body-count* will prove to be but a reflection of modern preconceptions on biology more so than an objective metric of one's sexual success.

It is not at all hard to witness the effectiveness of language in the study of the qualitative dimension. And yet, these no-great mysteries have run into a stumbling block which hilarity in ever presenting a stumbling block eludes the sense of humor of none but the modern speaker: there is no man who is courageous five and temperate six, or who possesses an above-average rationality quotient, or one hundred and twelve passion-units. Qualities such as the aforementioned few are not measurable (not in the numerical sense). They most certainly do exist, and they have been a part of language since language (as we know it) has been a part of mankind. However, in choosing to act upon the impulse to misapprehend that which he would not understand, in his negligence of complex reality, the living representative of modernity has forsaken his vocabulary in the name of his calculator.

The Walls of Pi

Two students were talking in a bar, one of whom was a sympathizer of mathematicians, and their discussion went like so:

---

[5] Though one could try to point to statistics relating IQ scores to income or poverty, committed crimes and testosterone levels, one could also purchase a duck-whistle for far less effort.

in a post on the internet that was meant to educate and to entertain, the illustrator of the comic was arguing in favor of mathematics in this way: there was an interview with a scientific journalist that had a similar character: there was once an argument between a mathematician and another scholar that took the following shape – *Kids who excel in math are usually apt with everything else*, said one scholar, *but it is rarely the other way around*, and he went on to speak of the higher IQ scores of mathematicians compared to common people; *science has accomplished more in a century than philosophy has in millennia*, said the scientific journalist; *but of course he's right!* said the student who, though not educated in mathematics, knew that to praise it was a proclamation of intellect; *unlike with philosophy*, the internet-artist argued, *nobody has gone to war over the square root of the hypotenuse.* All four discussions were interesting, to the superficial bystander, in that they asserted what had needed asserting all along – in the age of information, integers reign supreme! Another observer, however, having taken a minute to regain his footing, and admittedly still a little dizzy[6], agreed that they were interesting discussions indeed, but surely, so were unweeded gardens and dirty windows – and, surely, real satisfaction came from clearing them up.

As flattering as the above self-flattery is, it comes down to four arguments that in them contain more than the mere inner-boastings of their illocutionary purpose, for they make up four fundamental platitudes of the modern discourse: mathematicians are intellectually superior to the rest, hard sciences are the zenith of mankind, a man can be smart only if he agrees with this, and other disciplines of thought have proven detrimental to humanity. People seem to have accepted these so thoroughly, that, even if they will not explicitly state them as personal beliefs, they will find no reason for contention with any of the four statements upon intellectual subjection to their disclosure.

---

[6] Being dragged around in a circle tends to do that to a person.

These four arguments fused into one have become the default position of intellectuals and the average person alike. Even the student (and professor) of the humanities will but humbly plead: *yes, it is true, but where would we be without emotions?! Let us at least emotionalize (in an insufferably arrogant manner as is common for academia) while the student of nature reasons all there is to reason (sans sentiment)!*

And yet, as fundamental as the four ideas have become, there is also a fundamental wrongness in them: they are as fallacious as the contrived proverbs of popular theology, and as pleading as the most pathetic attempts at self-validation by representatives of the social sciences. To argue that mathematicians are more intelligent than non-mathematicians because of their IQ scores is to argue that statistics prove that numbers prove that statistically people who work with numbers have more numbers than those who have less. To say that science has accomplished more than philosophy is to say that the study of the natural world has told us more about the natural world than a study not concerned with the natural world has told us about the natural world. To believe that praising a science one does not understand makes one understand it more than others is to believe that finger-fishing in murky water increases one's chances of keeping all ten fingers. Finally, to take pride in the lack of wars started over the square root of the hypotenuse is to take pride in the lack of wars started over the right way to peel a banana. The argument for logical supremacy is not logically sound.

Nay, nor is it empirically sound either! For eugenicists have used the natural sciences to back their causes[7], natural sciences would not exist without philosophy of science[8], and people who have praised what they do not understand have hardly proven good examples in history. Even the statement of intelligence

---

[7] Including the eugenic wars of the 20th century;
[8] Or the philosophy that has made the democracies in which scientists have been free to study, research, and write;

among mathematicians – of the hard, measurable kind of intelligence (which is the real intelligence), the one that sets us apart from the rest of animalkind (and which sets mathematicians apart from the rest of mankind) has its empirical proof in dull accountants and incompetent teachers, and hardly genius of the likes that have made the world of IQ determinism distinct from the pre-IQ world in any valuable metric. The idolization of mathematicians is a scam through and through – it does not hold up in the real world, and it barely has the right to even venture out of the conceptual world, for it is too circular to stand even logical scrutiny, let alone reality.

But the issue I believe should concern us here is not the fallacy itself, as a mere cult of mathematics and sciences reliant on numbers, but the consequences resulting from it – the hegemony, if you will, of *integer before intellect*. With the advent of science, we have ironically come to know less about humanity than we used to, because we have willingly (and proudly) rejected what we used to understand. We have then tried to compensate for it by using this same fallacy, only to end up living according to rules that make a mockery of truth. We are stuck in a circular prison, by a circular argument, in a circular nightmare that culminates in our awakening to a cycle that cannot be broken, for we have lost our grip on the tools for its breaking; worse still, we have forgotten where they are, what they are, and if there ever were such tools in the first place.

<u>What is at Stake?</u>

Words are beginning to lose their meanings. Consequently, these meanings are being replaced with whatever can fill the vacuum. In an age where everything but absurdity is measurable, the void is being filled with a special kind of unmeaning. That should concern us. Words consist of 90% meaning and 10% sound.

Though we cannot yet tell what words are, it is scary to think they operate at only one-tenth capacity.[9]

First to go have been abstract notions. For instance, nobody knows what intelligence is (only that Einstein had 160 of it); nobody knows what a man is either – only that they are statistically stronger than women.[10] Soon, it will be less abstract things. We are already at war over the meanings of some. Finally, it will be the very material world that is at stake. It is not as farfetched as it sounds, for there are warning signs of this even as I write. It will no longer matter what money is, only that one has a lot of it – nor will it matter what it can buy, as long as whatever it buys costs a lot. I will ask the reader to imagine what happens when we forget the meaning of *human* (but remember that there are eight billion of us), and we lose touch with the meaning of *rights* (but remember that, multiplied by eight billion, their value might drop if distributed equally).

I do not warn of political consequence alone; politics has little to do with the true consequences. The real consequence is confusion, and whatever might come out of it will be as fire is to a nuclear explosion – inevitable, but not the subject one should fear the most. In a nuclear assault, even death is a secondary threat. What most of us fear are the horrors that happen to those who do survive the blast. The same applies to the confusion of which I warn. It is not just a problem that will (as it already has in isolated cases) lead to the immediate damnation of individuals, but, much worse, it will make the quality of life so negligible that the state of living will not differ from its opposite by any means worth mentioning. It is not by chance that a surge in depression, a pandemic of loneliness, and a zeitgeist of indifference have coincided with the spike in confusion. The plain of meaning has

---

[9] I do not suppose an appeal to inflation and the price of an image in words will make the economy of words sound even drearier.

[10] I dare the cock-sure reader to bring up the 'adult human male' definition and fail to anticipate the response.

become irradiated. The life of a mutant is not a happy life, the soil supports no plants, and our food is more toxic than it is nourishing – I will let the reader apply all three to the concept of meaning according to their preferences.

A Conspiracy Unmasked

This has already accounted for such consequences on culture as we can hardly see ourselves surviving, let alone correcting. Myself, I can barely hope to address them, though I write this essay precisely with that purpose – an essay, mind you, which I do not believe will be met by the eyes of many, and certainly not the minds that should most benefit from it.

Though how could it? One lacks the material means to make a change, and the effort exerted in the attempt is so devoid of the promise of profit, that, to the very people one hopes to reach, one is but a lazy slob, a malcontent, and a self-indulgent not-a-man stuck in a take so unscientific it cannot even be put to measure, let alone made to measure. Hardly capable of being counted, it does not belong on a table or spreadsheet or graph, nor does it find its place on either side of the equal sign (let alone the preferable side).

We have reached a point where the hope of a thought being made the subject of thinking has become a fool's hope.[11] We are approaching a development where, unless one toils exclusively for the purpose of improving one's finances, it will be better that one should remain lazy. It is already hard enough to create art and to learn for pleasure and to treat people kindly – now we must do it at a one-way risk to our finances. The person who has the lesser number (be it socially genetically or otherwise) is powerless against the person with the higher number (be it intellectually existentially or otherwise). How can one prove

---

[11] Though the hope of a fool being hired to think has become a reasonable expectation.

their worth to a man who can purchase all of one's property and all of their organs and still have enough left to pay journalists to report on the transaction?[12] Most of us cannot measure up to the worth a *Jaguar*. And until we've done something about this, the problems of which I speak will only worsen.

What is a man?
A collection of numbers.
What is a man lacking numbers?
He is less.

The appeal of high fantasy becomes evident when we consider the parallels, or the specific kind of hopelessness underlying the plot: the danger of war, the invasion of the orcs, the return of (malevolent) dragons… The Men of the West are weak, for they struggle in their inner rivalries, the dwarves have retreated to the mountains, hoping to be spared by isolation, and the less said about elves the better.

But there is a glimmer of hope. There always is. In fiction and in reality alike. One is that we have not been defeated (not yet), and, as entailed by the plurality of the pronoun, some of us have seen through the fallacy – I am certainly not the first, and, as I write my fifteen-page essay, there are people who have devoted thousands of hours of academic investment to the issue. Alliances are a good start. Another advantage is that, though we tend to differ on many things, the question that unites us is something on which we agree in full. Finally, and perhaps the best news of the bunch, is that the tools that can be employed to take down the prison (or at least its gates) are tools that we have at last found, and, better still, they are tools regarding which the enemy is not only powerless, but also oblivious – oblivious that they exist, oblivious that we have them, and oblivious that, once used, though he may not fall the same instant, his might will be irrevocably diminished.

---

[12] And, no doubt, spin it as a good thing.

I will here issue a disclaimer that the argument I present has nothing to do with the science of mathematics. I am in no way opposed to mathematics as a science – on the contrary, I believe there should be more of it in schools (provided it is taught well). Rather, what I aim to do is to speak in favor of language, and, as it happens, there is a numerical fallacy in my way. This fallacy, I stress again, is not mathematical science. It merely uses the latter as a weapon to bully its way into acquiring (and maintaining) its monopoly.

The monopoly in question is the titular prison. The metaphor of the prison is life as we know it, in all its inglorious calculations. The gate out of it, however, is not something that I can reliably open, for it is not up to me to do it, nor do I have the kind of ability necessary for the accomplishment of such an ambition. I can merely speculate a potential solution, and hope that those who try it, might at least put a dent on the lock, if not escape altogether.

I will again ask the reader to forsake any notions of competition between the sciences (linguistics versus mathematics and such), because, I assure you, my point is yet not what you think it is, and it is not a question of either of these two sciences. Keep in mind: though our surroundings may at times simulate one, we are not in an academic setting. We are navigating a prison, and pitting one science against another is an indulgent cockfight. Because neither the warden nor the prisoners nor the guards nor the crimes committed are themselves numbers. Rather, they are phenomena contingent on the arrogance of people who would have us convinced that dealing with numbers is tantamount to dealing with what can and cannot be, with how it should be, with what may or may not be said, and that which you must never try – not even try to think about. At their dreariest, the numbers themselves stand for the bars. Mathematics is merely metallurgy. My qualm has nothing to do with either metal or crafting metal – our problem is with tyrannical blacksmiths alone.

Another technicality to address is that this essay is not an allegory. It is best that the reader does not look at the points I make as something meant to apply to persons or events, general or specific, or to any particular ideology. The points I make do have determinate meanings, but their applicability is fluent. The structure of my essay is an informal criticism of the instant in history we currently inhabit; this is the only stipulation. As for which part of history, be it very recent history or history in the making, what people in history, be it people in power, people in academia, or the masses that outnumber both many times over, and what kind of inhabitance in history, be it the culture of the west, the modern experience worldwide, or our personal mental places where we draw conclusions, the applicability of the metaphor is up to the reader. As is the case with good fiction, there is an interpretation shared by both the writer and the reader, however, unlike in allegory, there is a part of the interpretation that belong solely to the intellectual faculties, preferences, and whims of the individual reader, and on which the writer has no right to impose his vision beyond a basic reminder that there is, after all, a shared meaning that both sides must respect. I do not consider this essay a difficult read, though it would behoove the prudent reader to read well-rested, so as to more fluently notice the shifts between directness and indirectness, and to read in good spirit, so as to interpret the latter with an open mind. The Cretan labyrinth was also a kind of prison, and, though I do not use a labyrinthine metaphor anywhere else in my essay, our way out might be reminiscent of its design. There will be twists and plenty of turns; and we would do well to keep track of them.

So where is the door then – or, rather, *what* is it? Well, I reckon, it must be the same door through which we entered. It is the same that we must exit if we seek to leave the prison. So let us first remember how we got here – surely, we can remember where the door is (and what it is) if we can remember our moment of entry.

Part 2. <u>Defining the Confines</u>

The Two Crimes

And as we do that, we must address a question that necessarily arises out of the fact of our arrival: we did not find ourselves entering the prison as free men. At some point prior, we must have been condemned. And at some point before that, we must have broken the law. It would be narcissistic of us to assume that we have all got stuck in prison as innocent men (it does happen in the real world, but the metaphor will not allow it here; in Pythagoras' prison, we are all guilty).

Our crime has been one of neglect, not dissimilar to neglectful parenting. It is like child neglect in the same way that child neglect is like an unpaid debt. Let me explain. We often hear that *our children are our future*. We must recognize this as the truism it is: like many of its kind, it is only half-true, and in this aspect, it is so only in the biological sense – otherwise, it is entirely false. I say this, because, on all levels except the genetic, our children are not our future. Even socially, once they have inherited our positions in their respective communal strata, the act of their inheritance will not be our future, but theirs. The only sense in which our children's succession of ourselves makes them our future is in the sense that, though we will be gone, our genes will yet live on through them: a part of our building-blocks (or at least the blueprint) will go on building after the current project has become vacant. And even so, the truth-value of the statement is only half, for unless we are willing to argue that we were the first instantiation of the genes we carry, the unavoidable conclusion is that, our children, in being our genetic future, are also our genetic past: in them we see not just our successors, but also our ancestors. Seen in this light, the subject sentence becomes clear: how is our crime similar to child neglect? It is similar in that we have neglected our past – tradition in which we live on in the same way as our ancestors have lived on, and, provided we maintain it, our children will one day join us. We have forgotten to nurture that, which, having once helped us find our way, has by the process of regeneration become frail in its rebirth, and now requires our assistance to nurture it back to strength. We have let go of the tradition of mind.

To put the metaphor in perspective, I am not accusing anyone of stupidity or anything of the like. Obsession with inherent mental power is a quirk of the other side, not mine. I merely point to absence of thought, not a disability. The man who has neglected his child is not a demented person; he is merely an absentminded person. He is also probably a lazy person, and, most certainly, a rather selfish person. We are in trouble not because our minds have failed us, but because we have failed our minds. When they spoke, we shut them up; and when they screamed, we got them drugged. That is bad parenting indeed.

In the non-symbolic world, that would be a criminal offense and a moral transgression. In the symbolic realm in which I use it, it is merely a form of character degradation. It is no less serious, but at least the only people who suffer are the perpetrators themselves. The selfish person who was not originally demented, has, by his own doing, acquired a kind of injury which effects could be likened to dementia. We have named our kids after our parents, but we have forgotten that we ever had parents.

Then, we have come to ask ourselves: who are these strangers we feel obliged to take care of? And why take care of them when we cannot even tell if we want them? Had they meant anything to us, surely, we would have named them after something that matters to us. This is slightly more literal than I had anticipated, but it is a coincidence on which I would do well to capitalize: there are many people whose names mean things their parents do not necessarily respect: I have met Sophies with familial indifference to wisdom, dishonest Emmetts, and effeminate Peters. Likewise, though we hold success and masculinity and intelligence and sanity and leadership as qualities of great importance, we have forgotten about their elaborate definitions;

we have flouted our obligation to learn them, and we hardly ever stop to think if they ever mattered. We have decided instead to explain them not as the meanings handed down to us, but as the meanings we can perceive within the limits of our contemporary experience, which, in its strict contemporaneity, is by definition weak: Sophia does not mean wisdom, silly; Sophia means that girl over yonder; now do not pester me with your wisdom, for I am a philosopher – and Sophie will be mine!

I am just as surprised at this as the reader: Pythagoras' prison was originally an asylum. We had become the stereotypical patient, ramming himself against rubber walls and calling out to who-knows-what (himself the least), hearing answers from who-knows-where (himself the best). What is a good man? It is a man who gives more than he takes! So a good man is a fool. What is a good man? It is a man who takes more than he gives! So a good man is a scoundrel. All the same, a good man is a bad man. So then what? Perhaps it is a man who gives as much as he takes? It must mean then, that a good man is a mediocre man. And what is an exceptionally good man? It is a man who is exceptionally mediocre! A good man is a smart man. A smart man will always adapt, whereas a stupid man will fail to adapt – and once the smart man has adapted to stupidity, he will have done such a good job at it, that to be first among idiots will be a sign of genius! With ramblings like these, it is no wonder that intellectual confinement was a necessity.

But the people meant to take care of us were also afflicted by madness. It was the same cause as ours, but with a slight alteration in symptoms. For they too had forgotten their ancestors, but worse than using names which meanings they do not know, they have opted to come up with new designations to hopefully conceal their lunacy. They no longer have to pronounce what they do not understand, but can instead utter words that they alone know. You will not hear these people cry out *Sanity!* and *Goodness!* and *Manhood!* They will instead say things like *Mental Health!* and *Success!* and *What?!* Unfortunately for them, a made-up word is only as good as a made-up world, and it is only in such a world that it can ever be valid. If our crime was like child neglect in the way that child neglect is like an unpaid debt, then their crime has been like forgery, in as far as forgery is like pleading insanity. It is a serious crime indeed. So how were they to avoid legal consequence? Simple. They built the prison and they made themselves wardens.

And to achieve this they have used a legal loophole to give themselves immunity from the meaning which loss had condemned the rest of us. They have validated their forged documents. Not attempting to destroy or to conceal this proof of their crime, they have argued like so, *Though we cannot call out to anyone with the names we have made up, at least not in the hope that anyone will respond, and though the documents we hold in our hands do not relate to persons, familiar or otherwise, our papers are yet real documents, for they relate to our dolls!* And so, the fake names became real by being assigned to fake persons, who in turn became real persons by virtue of their thusly acquired documents.

Sanity and Wisdom had been lost – but the doll of Mental Health was safely posed in the attic of the dollmaker, right next to the window where you can see her; and as Intelligence withered on a *Missing Persons* poster, Intellectual Quotient was being painted and polished and exhibited in the craftsman's shop. The neglected kids with their forgotten names had long since fled. Their ancestors with the forgotten faces had long since perished. The dolls with their doll names and wooden expressions are all accounted for. And they will live on for as long as craftsmen paint them and polish them and exhibit them in their shops.

Do not mistake this for pure and deliberate evil by the way. Whatever the wardens-to-be did with the dolls, they did it first out of fear, and then out of guilt. But that is not important just yet. All that matters at present is that they schemed and they scammed. Their troubled minds factor in only later.

It was not a complex ruse that they pulled off. On the contrary. It was a simple semantic swindle. First, a distinction was made between the confused many and their complementary few. They then sketched an equivocating picture between the forgotten reality and the freshly thought up fantasy.

Men and mannequins, provided the mannequins are advanced enough, differ very little, if at all, in regards to the measurable dimension. In shape and in size and in weight and even inside, they are both very similar. In the right lighting, and to the untrained observer, they are identical. As it stands, the names of dolls are like the names of people in that we do not necessarily know the meanings of either. The difference, however, is that the names of dolls can be given whatever meanings we want, and, you can rest assured, the made-up-person with the made-up-name will surely answer if we pretend it does, even though it is neither a person nor does it have a name.

So one side did not know what it was to which they called out – real or not, they could not tell. The other side did. It was most certainly not real, the subject of their appellation, but in being aware of this, their insanity seemed the lesser of the two. Though silence can be preferable to nonsense, the soundless vale is a maddening realm; apart from the deaf, everybody else would prefer something – even a whisper or a wail but preferably words; even if lies.

And so, the arbiter of meaning has become unmeaning. This is not a controversial claim. Note that numbers in isolation have no semantic value. There is nothing to the number seven unless we assign to it the concepts of an antonym of thirteen, the height of the brown bear in imperial units, or the days of the week – nor does twenty-four hours mean a day unless we have first decided what a day is and whatever an hour is supposed to be. One could call it the interval between sunrises codified for social function.

Another might say it is the time in which a person's period of activity goes through its stages of awakening, action, and rest. It could also be a phrase to indicate a completion of a fixed period, be it literally or figuratively. All the same, you would not call a day twenty-four, nor is a week a one-hundred-and-sixty-eight. Measurement does not tell us anything about what we measure unless we know what it is that we are trying to measure – both the object *and* the property. So to argue that a concept is believable just because it is backed by numbers is to say that a concept means what it means whenever it has no meaning.

But there is one pragmatic advantage to having a numbered system of reality that makes the aforementioned hurdle but a minor setback, provided it can even rise in significance enough to be considered a setback. It is the fact that, once understood as the definitive paradigm, numerical systems of measure cannot fail. Though the measurement may fail, the system itself is never in danger. Nobody wonders *are we wrong in our pursuit of a number?* They merely assert, *we have the wrong number!* and go on to blame either the instrument or the operator. Because, they know, a number is most certainly the answer; we just need to find the right one, and there is an infinity of options through which to search. Circular walls are impenetrable.

Notice how often the western world has undergone changes in its dominant religions.[13] Shortly after man became the apex entity on Earth, animals lost their divinity (with the possible exception of the housecat). The taming of the elements ensured that fire and water were too impersonal to rule over humans. The anthropogenic immortals of the previous era have come and gone as a new hope followed each episode of disillusion. When native-born Ares failed to protect, Danubian Heron took his place. Wherever Jove proved treacherous, some other cult would step up.

---

[13] I am only using this as an example. The essay does not address either organized religion or personal beliefs. I mean no offense; the examples that follow are thoroughly simplified accounts.

Eventually, the gods that should have been visible but were never seen became replaced by a deity that is not visible but has nevertheless been seen. In time, the religion that taught that *charity shall cover the multitude of sins* was shown to have been mistaken as charity failed to cover even the power bills. It was atheism that followed as the dominant conviction, as men began to realize that no god is better than gods who play favorites. But as the theory of no souls and no minds began (for some inexplicable reason) to show a tendency for soullessness and mindlessness, so did this new age adopt a worldview it had promptly named after an even newer age, one full of soul and in enmity with the egoic mind, which, forwarded by egoic minds, has now given way to a myriad of smaller faiths, each different to its predecessors in some way, be it superficial or essential, and looking for the truth with its own unique or derived methods, in an attempt to reiterate and reanalyze and explain the mysteries of the world as they manifest in such things as existence, in goodness, in joy, and in suffering.

Contrast this to the cold, mathematical understanding of reality forwarded by the modern spirit, and you will see how the patterns resemble one another, but also how they differ in favor of the latter. The fluctuations in thought regarding science and all things reasonable appear to occasionally undergo changes, yet the more they change, the more they stay the same.

No sooner was positivism abandoned than it become the next big thing. No sooner did intelligent people begin to question the validity of IQ testing than IQ testing became the unquestioned metric of human intelligence. Just as we learned that eugenics is wrong and evil and really not even worth considering, we were taught that evil is not real and a rebranded form of eugenics just might save the world. It used to be that the rich would say that money is the be-all and end-all of existence as they took away everything you owned. Now, it is their children who tell you that money is not everything in life as they proceed to take away everything you own. As you can see, there is a traceable change and even the semblance of reevaluation, but ultimately it is just the same swindle iterated anew.

The effect gives off the illusion of objective self-criticism as well as the illusion of consistency. The warden is humble enough to admit (some of) his mistakes, however, his failure is never a failure in thinking or theory or heaven forbid conviction. The only error is an error *under* the system, for an error *of* the system is out of the question. If I measure a ten-kilogram object at nine kilograms, the mistake is mine – the International System of Units remains faultless. This is understandable, seeing as weight can be presented in numbers. Then again, if I measure a sociopathic misfit as a successful man and a genius, you would not say that the mistake must have been the number with which I came up, as opposed to the fact that it was a number in the first place. Yet, some people will. Though there is no number to test things like sanity or achievement,[14] there is an infinity of numbers with which to try, and a surplus of fools to take up the challenge. Some will even argue that success and intelligence are factors independent from not being a sociopathic misfit, all in the name of preserving the number. I can tell that they are mistaken, because nobody would argue the same thing in other contexts, for example, that good eyesight is independent from being able to see well.

Now, I can imagine the attempt to refute this: *good eyes can be medically tested, whereas success is not!* Though I do not hold that as a contradiction to what I have said, but a complement. Because you would not, in lieu of medical data, judge a person's eyesight to be good or bad based on his wealth. Nor would you try to shoehorn a correlation between the two. You would instead come up with a method to gauge his ability to see things, and in turn you will have created a rudimentary eye exam. It is seeing well that corresponds with the medical reality of good eyesight. So why is the check for success then not the equivalent of seeing well? It is as if we have so lost faith in concepts that are not measurable, that we have come to replace them with loosely assigned correlatives that are. The pursuit for meaning has been likened to the religious sloppiness from two paragraphs above:

---

[14] ... including intelligence, as you will see in the next essay;

delusional nuttery in search for something that does not exist. But since we still experience things like existence, goodness, suffering and joy, and we dream of success, we remain desperate for a way to explain them. Disillusioned by the semantic flux, we are presently seeing the man of numbers, in his immovable philosophy, holding up a scale and asking that we hand them over for measurement. *After all, he argues, Why change the car just because the steering wheel is broken, when we are in the right lane anyway?*

The Old Code and the New Deal

Now, remember that, as neither Pythagoras nor the prison nor the crimes are literal things, neither does my evocation of persons juxtaposed to dolls point to a debate on humanity,[15] but to ideas. Our ancestors were the age-old ideas we had forsaken, and our neglected children were those same ideas as we failed to develop them in our own mental traditions. The metaphor is admittedly flexible, but its conceptual scope is invariably rooted in thought. The mannequins are the intellectual validation of whatever we made up to replace what we had lost.

Men, just like the ideas we have inherited, are not like dolls because men are alive. What I here reference as living ideas are also alive in the sense that made up ideas are not. The former are passed down in history, they are molded by experience, and become renewed in the spontaneity of the human intellect. The latter are created on the spot, shaped to always fit a preset schematic, and, safe from the tumults of time, are kept twitching in the isolated circles of their coinage – at times made popular, at times stored aside, but without exception estranged from human sense. Neither are the names of men like the names of dolls, for the former can call back, whereas the latter do not even live up to the occasion of muteness. At their most advanced, they can

---

[15] Although it will steer that way two essays from the present;

merely imitate, and the best we can do with them is pretend. My name is not my name because somebody gave it to me, but because I have accepted it. I have discovered some part of who I am to be reflected in what they call me – etymological, historical or otherwise, it was a fact of perception that did not contradict reality. Likewise, concepts that ring true cannot be captured by just any conceptual framework; one must toil to discover them and refine them and explain them. Concepts analogous to dolls, however, can be called whatever one wants to call them, and explained with whatever string of words suits the person that makes them. The doll will not object, and neither will the fantasy that it consents.

Life is the quintessential factor in all cases: it is life as we understand it intuitively, life as we learn it empirically, and life as it has, historically, opposed the abyss of time better than even ancient (refurbished) mannequins. This goes literally as well as figuratively. Though we are able to look upon Shakespeare's house in Stratford upon Avon,[16] it is not the relic, but his life that we celebrate – of what he did with it, how much he accomplished while he had it, and how, in his legacy, what one sees is life's abundance through history: not the wealth of Rome or the Pyramids of Egypt, but the pride of Caesar and the conflict in Brutus and the insufferableness of Cleopatra. It is the same with living ideas – the words of real things. It is pointless to wonder about the mental health of Richard III, but there is much to say regarding his sense of guilt; there is little information about his intellectual quotient, but one's awe at his cunning has lived far longer than psychological quackery. Neither is the rot in Denmark a stench in the country's GDP. Ghosts haunt the living; they do not steal their wallets. It has always been about life and the living. Living justly no less. Even before the progenitors of western theology saw a parallel between sin, filth and death, pagan mythologies have been in pursuit for the waters of eternal life.

---

[16] This refers to the house where he was born; the house where he lived has been torn down.

But life cannot be measured![17] the wardens will argue. And measurement is just too important to let go. For one, it does away with reading and learning and interdisciplinary humdrum that is but so much wasted time. Philosophy? *Pah!* It is the least productive pastime since skeet-shooting. Contemplation makes of the answer an elusive beast, one that calls for a wild and dangerous hunt, whereas post-Neolithic society prefers its prey domesticated. The debate has been settled: a bird in the bush (nay, not the bush, by the sky!) as opposed to infinite specimens of the renowned dodo-bird, as it jumps in the sailors' pot to warm itself. There has not been an easier choice since *what's for dinner* in the sixteen hundreds.

Measurement is the safest metric – the only metric that tells us something about something else without any room left for doubt or debate or debacle. Why posit a theory in danger of disagreement – of speculation – of arguments and of rebuttals and of questions and answers and (if it comes to it) minds being changed: of immeasurable things having immeasurable effects without measure? Why, a word for a word makes the whole world loud! Puppets, on the other hand… puppets are quiet. They are safe. They are changeless unless we change them ourselves, which is to say unless we want to. They do not move and they do not speak (unless preprogrammed to say what they will), and they will always fit to measure.

So what a triumph for science shall it be, focused on the static half of reality as it is, if it could immobilize the other half as well? If all fell silent before it; if the world agreed that they must agree? If none came before us and none came after, if we could maintain a tenseless equilibrium, if all could be counted and consequently predicted, if life as we know it became as automatic as one number following the next: if X at t was always X at t, and for all

---

[17] If there is a halfwit in the room, let him say *you can measure life in years!* to reveal himself now or forever hold his peace.

the *t*s and all the *X*s, the only difference were one of quantity –
if the only description made could be fit on a graph?

Toys will be as men and men will be as toys. Yes, it is a
versatile metaphor. Disagreement will be as but a talking doll
short-circuiting. What we used to call lies will be no different
than the product of the honorable toymaker, and protesting
humans but rogue mannequins. Consider how much of this you
see in popular philosophy of mind. It is all relative. Knowing the
particles means knowing the person.

Numbers have become the be-all and the end-all of cognitive
licenses, the immeasurable has been denied its value, and the
arbitrary has been counted into authority. It no longer matters
that one can tell apart an automaton form a human being; it only
matters that both can be given the same names: productive, net
positive, dispensable.

Prison Security

So now, that we have had a look around the prison, and that we
have finally found the gate, having been reminded of our former
crime (and just as importantly the crime of the wardens), we
remain facing the fundamental task without which our efforts so
far will have proven in vain: we need to get out! There is no point
in finding a gate that remains forever closed. We have might as
well run up into another wall. So how do we do it? We cannot
simply walk out, for we are serving a collective sentence; until the
majority have reformed, we cannot hope to become free men. Keep
in mind, the metaphor is of society, and social changes do not just
happen. They need a mass of likeminded people, and they require
resources. We cannot sneak out for the same reason.

I will first warn you that there is no point arguing with the
guards. They will not listen. A man who has spent enough time
looking at dolls will begin to find real people uncanny. Like dolls,

real people look humanoid, but, unlike dolls, they are too unpredictable to be set free. *Freedom of movement is off-limits but to the immobile*, the guard thinks, *for the agile mistake their legs for a license to walk!* The gatekeepers of modern thought have become so used to the static and the predictable, that now, that their bosses have canonized mannequins, they find humanity alien: it is human children that are a threat to the dolls, for they might break them, it is human individuality that is a transgression, for its kinks cannot be mended, and it is human names that refer to nothing in particular, for they fall on deaf ears. So think the educators and the professors (meaning those who profess) and the professional analysts who carry out independent research resulting in independent discoveries that all come to the same conclusions. It is irrelevant that it sounds crazy. It only matters that they can enforce it. Which is why they will keep doing it. They must, lest they forfeit their relative liberties. If you released all the inmates, the only people left inside would be those employed to remain there. It is only by the oppressed that the guards can feel privileged.

Perhaps talking to the wardens might make things right, but let us not fool ourselves. It was them that turned the asylum into a prison in the first place. Were they competent, they would have set us straight a long time ago, and, were they reticent, they would have released us on account of wasting everybody's time. Instead, they only work to bolster the fences. They have a lot to gain keeping us where we are. For one, as long as we are enshrouded in our mutual confusion, they can remain in possession of what the world considers sanity. No, they do not need to define sanity for that – they do not even care for the word. They only need to replace it with *mental health* and phrase the definition so that, far from a synonym to sanity, it merely restates that the best slave is a happy slave: all ye depressed and angry and kin of the malcontent must remain in the madhouse forcefully, and all ye jubilant may remain there blissfully.

I wish I could point to individuals or at least to delimited groups of individuals who could stand for the wardens, but the fact of the matter is that there is no such ideal scapegoat. Unlike that of the guards, the individual personhood of the wardens is metaphorical. In reality, the wardens represent all of us whenever we look upon the fact of our enslavement and choose to deal with it by any method other than addressing it for what it is. Some of us run to what the internet may recognize as the syllable that within its three sounds can cover the entirety of the free time the average person utilizes in the span of their lives: cope. Others may try to come up with justification for it, to explain away the fact of our enslavement as normal, or to alternatively pay a professional to do it for them by the session. Why else argue that one trips because one cannot adapt the length of one's pace – that the chains around one's ankles have nothing to do with it? Maybe because acknowledging the chains means acknowledging the need for their breaking. And moral interaction is just too much work. A polished mannequin is less offensive to the senses than a screeching brat. The reader should now understand why I said the wardens were crushed by guilt as they went through with their scam. Just as kids play with dolls and madmen indulge in their own ramblings, the dolls we built were originally a coping mechanism.

We are all part-warden. It is how the warden appears to outnumber us, even though he is the minority. Hence the plurality in my text. As a phenomenon he is one, but he is one of many, and one in charge of most. I am sure the reader remembers that the wardens made the prison to escape the law – to put behind bars people guilty of the same crimes as those who had the institution built. It is quite the petty game we play: to make ourselves look good by the people we condemn. To make ourselves feel sane compared to the rest. Others do the same thing in return. In concept, I am a warden and a prisoner of many. To the indifferent, I am a warden who confines them for their indifference; to these same people, I am also an inmate confined for disturbing the peace.

Do not mistake this for mere reflection or similar hypocrisy. It is not quite as ignoble. It is merely an attempt to make sense of the world. To render frustration reasonable. We have lost our wits. We are correct to recognize that others too have lost theirs. It is only right that we feel there is something wrong. What is not right is the system we are trying to utilize to change this. Instead of looking for the sense we have lost, we look at paychecks and grades and IQ scores and bodycounts and age and stature and net worth and credit score to argue for proof of our success. We look at whatever we have called science and whatever passes as fact to make our case. Our ignorance comes second to our convictions. Once we have understood that we have so succeeded, we determine a system and we go on to attack those who oppose it. Not because it is a good system, but because we can call ourselves successful only as long as it keeps us that way. That is the proto-history of Pythagoras' prison. It was just a bunch of people counting to avoid thinking, and a few more counting to make themselves count. The rest were just the common human factors that took over the construction of our babbling tower: social inertia, social entropy, conservation of the masses... free radicals, negative charges, decadent neutrons. You know how it is. Marley's ghost has got tied up in a chain reaction.

The Inmates

So, at last, we might try to turn around and talk to the other inmates as equals. Brother to brother. At the least, we will have made some good friends along the way. Sure, let us pretend that making friends in this age really is that easy. But whichever opinion we hold regarding socialites, let us not forget that a friendly smile frames a treacherous snout. No sooner will you open up to a fellow inmate than he will rat you out to the warden.

I wish I could say that a close alliance with the multitudes is the answer. That fraternity unlocks liberty. On occasion, I wish that I still believed that to be the case. Alas, on those occasions I wish that I had not once believed it to be the case so passionately that

I have since been reminded of Blake's opus. Experience is ever in enmity with idealism. The best one can hope for in the kind of inmate with whom one is most likely to converse is fleeting agreement in one moment followed by what I will choose to diagnose as horrible memory the next. But not to deride our equals too much, the disillusion they cause is not a tragedy without a moral. There is much to learn from intellectual relapse, especially in regards to the numerical fallacy. In particular, the motive in its propagation. The observation is most visible in that facet of life that is communal but not bonding, aging but hardly maturing, and vivid but seldom lively – I am talking, of course, about social life, in particular, the experience of trend one shares with one's peers. The two trends in which I intend to trace it are conversations on wealth and casual powerlifting, of which neither has had its debut all that recently, however, the fact of their very recent comeback is an excellent example of what I have argued so far.

Concerning the former, I have been as of late exposed to people whose philosophy in life seems to be *I am morally obliged to be rich*. They are not wealthy people (I'd say generally middle class) and they do not even have the kinds of jobs that could make them particularly wealthy. They just hold to the opinion that they must have money. To make matters more bizarre, these are not your typical lovers of mammon, nor are they the type to flaunt their wealth on any occasion. They merely put the ideal of money before anything else. In regards to character and the economic spectrum, they borrow from both its extremes. As a poor person lives paycheck to paycheck, they live paycheck for paycheck; as a rich person buys an expensive overpriced car, they buy cheap overpriced cars; and as a high class person buys fancy food from private vendors, they buy fancy brands at supermarkets. Although, like poor people, they complain they cannot afford much, unlike poor people, they spend a lot of money; and although, like the rich, they boast of how much money they make, unlike the rich, they do not actually make a lot of money. They are not averse to crime – but only if it gets them ahead. Nor are they opposed to intellectual conversation – as long as it can get them ahead. They are not hedonists. They can, on occasion, stand behind an idea and even believe it. The first clause of the idea, of course, is that one cannot see it through without money – be it patriotism or environmentalism or innovation, they must have a lot of money before they can do anything with their beliefs. Ask them if they would do a petty crime, and watch them recoil in disgust. Speak of the crimes of a wealthy man, and prepare to hear his defense.

The other trend is that of lifting ridiculously heavy weights, which its adherents argue is sometimes for health and sometimes for ego and sometimes for strength, and which seems to me is mostly for nothing. These were the first bodybuilders I had encountered that did not give a damn about form. They can be skinny or obese or struggling with that unfortunate corporal dualism known as skinnyfat. They can look at an excellently built man and consider him weak because he lifts light, or speak of a historical war hero and call him *a woman* because he did not lift at all (I have personally witnessed this; to add to the irony, the girl who said it, as far as I have been able to discern, is also a woman). They will speak of the health benefits of powerlifting while bulking on cheeseburgers. They will warn against ego-lifting but they will not miss an opportunity to flex for social media. The cherry on top, though they will have you convinced they adore the gym, they will stop going as soon as the fad is over.

In as far as the first group does not understand the concept of money, and the second group has divorced fitness from being fit, my statement that words are losing their meaning is once more shown to apply to the present confusion. But that is not why I bring them up. There is something more profound than contradiction in these examples of ignorance. They are examples of inmates turning into wardens. They are misunderstandings of value (one of purpose, the other of vaguely biological qualities), and numbers are added to cover it up. In the case of the former, it is wealth, measured in number, that determines right from wrong: a good product is an expensive product, a thing to praise is the possession of wealth, and a thing to dread is the lack of wealth; the immorality of a crime or the morality of an agenda is determined by its prospective revenue. There is no point risking being wrong or right when you can be wrong or rich instead. In the case of casual powerlifting, it is weight presented in numbers that settles the question of value (or masculinity or strength or some such). One does not need to go through the trouble of contemplating the value of man, and then compare it to the values in a given man (himself not least) when one can simply look at the number on the plate to tell everything they need to know of this man: is it higher or lower than it is pleasing?

The same goes for aesthetics. It is not a coincidence that many still pretend the golden ratio has solved the question of beauty. Or that the alternative are statistics on *this many women would*. It is not for an understanding of aesthetic theory that the most desirable qualities in men and women are believed to be directly measurable metrics. Why reflect on one's own tastes to determine attraction; why regard the contours of the face, complexion, shape, individual and holistic, why think about nuances in mannerism, or the expressiveness in the eyes... when one can simply look at bust and height and settle the question for good. One does not need to know anything about technology to buy the computer mouse with the higher DPI or the CPU with the higher clock speed. This same customer will be happy to know that the piece of hardware with the higher number is also the more expensive of the lot. Judging character to determine if a person would make a good employee? *Why bother when three years of experience should suffice? No? How about five?* Presented with a political development in a country with which one is not familiar, one is likely to look at its wealth to determine its worth. Some would also check the nation's average IQ scores to tell if its inhabitants are properly human. After all, learning about countries is only for the unlearned. The properly ignorant understand that numbers are the true substitute for history. Though keep in mind that official history has been tailored to mirror those same numbers. *Have you heard of that poor country with horrible IQ records and no historical feats we care to report? You agree they sound perishable, yes?*

This is what I had in mind when I warned of a *truly negative impact* whenever a fallacy escapes academia and spreads among the masses. It is the normalization of lunacy. I call it lunacy because it is the opposite of reason: it discourages thought; it dumbs down reality; it cheapens intellect. And it is no longer constrained to experimental facilities like philosophical institutes, discussed in colleges and withering away in papers nobody reads and citations everybody lists. No, it has become inference itself; it has replaced philosophy. And nobody cares to discuss it. The danger in it is the same as the danger of any system of thought that has done the same or threatens to do the same, and it has been echoed through history so much that the reader should be able to determine it on their own.

Still, there is power in being able to recognize the fallacy. There is virtue in calling it out. Truth be told, that is the gist of our battle. So, rather than looking at inmates and thinking *a-ha! the key to liberty!* try to look upon them and think *yes, people in need of liberation*, and figure out your approach from there.

Just beware of the capos. Capos, for those who don't know, are privileged prisoners that help the prison guards.[18] They are most certainly inmates, and they are by no means free – some of them do not even have very special privileges at all; they are just there to feel special and to make the job of the guards easier. These are people who have bought into the narrative – to the point where they do not even see the prison – only the mad around them and the mad above them, and, in between, on the chain that they mistake for a climbing rope, they see their ambition to ascend.

---

[18] They appear historically in the 1940s in the bleakest context for the setting. The term used here is not intended to reference the historical capos beyond the function described in the main text.

Part 3. <u>A Way Out</u>

<u>Not an Easy Way</u>

Faced with indifference, treachery and mockery, one might get the impression that there is, in fact, no way out. But our situation is not quite as dreary: there most certainly is a way; the catch is that it is not an easy one. Because even if we could convert the indifferent, weed out the traitors, and shut up the mockers, be it hypothetically or even magically, there still remain before us a locked gate, impenetrable walls, and undiggable tunnels. I wish that, to this, I could simply say that *salvation is within us* and be done with it. I would remain (technically) right, considering the identity of the wardens does suggest a potentially introspective approach. With that said, our goal is to escape, not to become enclosed in yet another confine, namely ourselves. That would only serve to make us happy slaves (or starved ones, depending on how far we choose to retreat). Besides, escaping *within ourselves* in mind while our bodies remain within the territory of our captors will leave our barely conscious selves at the whims of whoever happens to pass by. That will not turn out well for us. The people in this prison have bullying tendencies. The guards most of all. You either fight back or you have your passivity witness to your consent. Then again, if you have been following the metaphor, you can probably tell that fighting the enemy head-on is just as pointless, as none of them possesses the key. Though we might come out victorious in theory, the struggle will be tantamount to trying to harvest a lawn for food.

But our hope for a way out lies precisely in those two facts: that the guards are bullies, and that they can't get out either. If we ask ourselves *why is that the case* in regards to both statements, and if we honestly pursue the answers, by the time we have satisfied our curiosity, we will have made a viable plan of escape. It is not an easy plan, and it is by no means perfect; but it is certain to work if we can only put our minds to it.

One might be tempted to call the two sides *the natural* sciences and *the humanities*, but that would be misleading. It would be akin to calling the Second World War a war between people with atmospheric symbols on their uniforms and people who prefer celestial symbols outside the solar system. It is in reality a struggle of a much deeper reach that happens to coincide with a visible distinction on the superficial level.

The problem is not that two kinds of sciences (or a science and a pseudoscience) struggle for domination. It is rather a conflict of convictions, and it just happens that one conviction has chosen as its representative the field with which it is easier to manipulate. The field that, much like the German uniforms in the Second World War, is cold and unitary and with a sense of fashion that reeks of an assumed superiority, and, also like the German uniforms, believes it has a claim on the will of God. Although, ultimately, like these same uniforms, it is merely a garment, and it has no significance past that. You either like the fashion, or you don't. The other side is also compatible with the analogy. Just like the allies in the Second World War, with their varied uniforms and tactics and just as varied beliefs, the humanities do not have one method and one set of convictions alone – not even a shared conviction on how to go about forming them. In fact, just as some countries that sided with the allies were in reality Fascist, so are some branches of the humanities devoted to serving the natural sciences. As such, the diverse humanities present a body much harder to rally behind a single banner than the side that is all about uniformity and not at all about morality. I repeat, the specific sciences are a matter of representation, not the actual debate. So whenever you see a discussion that tries to pit one field against another, just remember that you are merely looking at a portrait of a battle, and, although you can tell a lot from a good portrait (literally, *the whole picture!*) it is only a single frame out of many.

But not to carry the militaristic imagery too far, it is really not about a war waged as much as collaboration – as I mentioned in the exposition: the spirit has already invaded codified thought; humanities do not clash with the natural sciences – rather, humanities and natural sciences alike have come to worship a philosophy that is not. You do not see biologists teaching linguists about cells, nor do you see linguists teaching biologists about syntax. What you do see are mathematicians telling biologists what syntax is, and later these same biologists telling linguists about the syntax they found in ultrasonic vocalization among rats, which results in linguists telling philosophers that language is not a human thing after all. To this, you hear the philosopher say *we knew all along!* Next, you see sociologists teaching society about hell, and psychologists profiting madly. To complete the cycle, we are currently experiencing economists practicing applied sociology.

You see, the point was never about what science says, or even which science says it. It was about what a certain fluke of philosophy asked science to confirm. The fluke in question, you may find, is none other than the bully who felt stupid in class, harassing the smart kids after the lecture.

<u>*A Note on Bullies*</u>

The bullying dynamic between the two modes of thought, i.e. of the subjugator and the subjugated, should be easy to demonstrate. Whereas one is certain and cannot be questioned, the other exists only because the former still tolerates it. Whereas making fun of natural scientists is the mark of ignorance, making fun of philosophers is the mark of true science. And whereas men of numbers use numbers to prove themselves right, men of the word have become so insecure by the dynamic, that they too use numbers to prove their science, to themselves not least.

The portrait of bullies and the bullied goes far. It extends to the point that the latter are beginning to form their internal groups wherein they bicker among themselves in their own hierarchies based on the standards of coolness they fail to meet outside their society; much like the mini-cliques that form in middle schools among the bullied: reacting to the dominant cliques, living in fear of the dominant cliques, and living to imitate the dominant cliques in their own isolated circles. Men of words, afraid to stand up to abuse, have decided to mask the fact with method. No longer daring to argue for the veracity of qualitative assessment, they either deny objective reality altogether, at which point they degrade their craft to total nonsense, or they try to infuse it with quantitative models, at which point they degrade their craft to subtotal nonsense. And so they pay their homage, lease their validation, and keep up an arrogant kingship to cover for their serfdom.

But there is a deeper truth to the observation than this comment, and it is the notion that bullies, be it literal schoolyard bullies, semi-literal political bullies, or their parallel institution in academia, are all fearful creatures: afraid of the outside world, and terrified by its challenges, they go on to build a barrier against the reality they fear. When a bully feels stupid in class, he does not beat up the nerds during recess because he is strong. He does it because strength is all he has, and because he must prove to himself that it is all that matters.[19] I admit he is a fearsome beast, but for all the big charts and complex algorithms and impressive research and diplomas and intimidating jargon, despite the white lab coats and bespectacled professors scribbling overlong formulae on green blackboards behind test tubes, and all the name-calling and the belittling and ostracization and mean looks from an elevated point of view, no less grand than it is gross, the sight before us remains but a cowardly middle schooler, too scared to admit that he felt stupid, and too proud to try and do better next time.

---

[19] I am of course simplifying the phenomenon for the sake of brevity.

Not too long ago, I witnessed a discussion between two people I will here refer to as my friends. One of them was a very nice fellow (he still is) with a passion for the natural sciences, and an unfortunate confusion regarding their scope: that the methods of studying nature should dictate the handling of all things human. He was talking about a research (carried out I don't know where) in which people were asked the question (I'm paraphrasing): _would you be more hurt if your partner cheated on you sexually, or if they fell in love with another person (platonically)?_ The survey had shown that most men chose the first option (sexual infidelity) and most women chose the second (platonic love) as the thing that would hurt them more were it to happen to them in a relationship. In this, my naturalist friend saw something profound concerning the biological reality of the sexes: men, obsessed with passing down their genes, could not bear the thought of their mate being possibly impregnated by the genes of another; women, on the other hand, obsessed with raising the offspring they have already _gened_, need a good provider and protector by their side, and so, quite indifferent as to whether or not their partner has used some of his genes on another mate, are more concerned about his emotional attachment to them, without which they risk being left without a provider and protector. The other person, this one an emergent master of psychology yet to study about the psychological faults of arrogance, argued that the research paper suggests nothing of the sort: _there can be cultural reasons for those results,_ he argued (I'm paraphrasing), _such as men being brought up in cultures that make fun of the cuckold, and women being brought up in cultures that force them into emotional competition with one another,_ which would explain the variation in the answers.

I don't think either makes much sense. To clarify, they certainly do make _some_ sense, but we must remember that _some_ is a scalar antonym of _a lot._

The Darwinianist's response[20] begs the question. It begins with an obsession with genes only to conclude an obsession with genes, which it later uses as proof of obsession with genes. The question posed was not *what would make you less confident in the plausibility to see your genes carried into the next generation?* The question was *what would hurt you more?* Offspring were not the subject of the survey. It could refer to couples that do not want children, teenage couples who usually don't or homosexual couples who generally can't, and the cheating affair could be just a fling, the result of which is seldom the begetting of offspring. I do not suppose a man who answered he would be devastated were he to find out his heterosexual partner was cheating on him would be much relieved to learn that she merely practiced oral or anal sex with the subject of her affair. *Whew, so she was not trying to get pregnant by him! What good news!* nor would he feel any better if he already had five grown up children with this same woman, all his. *Well, what's just one night now that I've already spread my genes, eh? She can' even get pregnant at her age anyway!* At this point, a person with obsessively-genetic convictions would most likely say that what we feel is rarely in a one-to-one relation with reality. *The act of cheating entails the attempt at pregnancy on a primordial level,* he would explain, *That the way it was executed cannot make the other person pregnant has nothing to do with how we've been hardwired to react to the very thought that it might have, were it carried out differently.* Intention goes completely out the window for the Darwinianist; what one feels is just as irrelevant, unless it proves the theory of obsessive genes – at which point both intent and emotion become absolutely relevant to the discussion. If a man feels sad because he found out his child is not his, the intentionality of his emotion will be proof of the obsessive gene theory. If he was sad because he felt betrayed, then the obsessive gene theory will rule out intentionality as unreliable. As I said, unless we presume it, we cannot conclude it. It is a dogmatic

---

[20] Let us call it that for convenience.

argument. It eliminates all other explanations on principle, and concludes that its own explanation is the only one – on principle. This is hard science.

I cannot support the cultural explanation either. While it does not beg the question like the alternative before it, and so it does not jump to a similar conclusion, in the words of Sayers' Lord Peter Wimsey, it does not "even crawl distantly within sight of a conclusion" (Ch. 4). It takes nothing out of the research, and it makes no claims other than that nothing can be taken out of it.

That culture shapes the way we feel about things is a truism I do not dispute, then again, the nature of the answers suggests that we live in a culture just balanced enough that culture should not factor in to an overwhelming degree: in an extremely patriarchal society, if you asked a man how bad he would feel if his partner cheated on him, he would probably reply, *Why should I feel bad? It is her that is about to lose her head*; conversely, in an extremely gynocentric society, if you asked a man how he would feel if his partner fell in love with another, he would probably shrug it off, *As if she ever loved me in the first place*. Furthermore, for all the appeals to cultural relativity one can make, there is a point one positively cannot obscure with such doubt, and it is the fact that every culture disapproves of infidelity.[21] Moreover, every culture looks down on men who would willingly subject themselves to cuckoldry. Upon discovering a love affair, men do not tend to differ a lot across cultures. Sure, the pressure to divorce your partner may be cultural – the urge to strangle them (their lover included) is most likely not. Towards the feminine argument, I will add that, in a healthy civilized society, any person whom nobody can love would be a person that nobody would want – I repeat, *any person*, not just women made to compete with other women; the unlovable not being loveable is not culture – it is

---

[21] Save for perhaps some isolated pockets in modern western culture. The fact that this exception exists in a distinctly amoral society is further proof that any moral society shuns disloyalty in marriage.

tautology. I would not want to learn that my wife does not love me any more than I have wanted to learn that my brothers conspired to kill me. The pain of ultimate rejection is unisex and universal.

So the Darwinianist has said nothing of value, and the psychologist has said nothing at all. And yet, there most certainly is something to conclude from the research and the answers provided. It is not at all hard to do once one has done away with preconceptions concerning the nature of the inference, or the assumed obligation that it must refer to the sexes as opposed to individual characters. The thing to conclude from the survey is that half of the people who took it are more likely to justify cheating.[22] It would take a bona fide idiot to overlook the enormity of an actual affair compared to a mere platonic desire, strong though it may be. Committing murder in the heart has far lesser consequences than committing murder in the real world – I am sure even Christians will agree. So how comes it then that half the people who took the survey answered in opposition to this logic? It could be that, *Sure, I cheated, but it's not like I did something all that bad, honey – do you not know that real pain is when your partner actually falls in love with somebody else? And I have done nothing of the sort. Cheating is but a fling.* Conversely, it could be that, *I know you cheated babe, but it was a one-time-thing, that totally makes it better – at least you still love me, right?*[23]

Humans are weird like that. When we say things, we do not merely reveal a single string of information per sentence. Rather, we oblige ourselves to many truths (or things we hold to be true) by the proposition. We state our convictions. We channel our experiences. We project what we have done and what we are likely to do and what we expect to think and feel about it. It is

---

[22] I repeat, irrespective of their gender.

[23] These can also be in the third person, as in justifying the actions of a person one tries to defend, such as a family member or a friend; the two I have written above do not exhaust all of the possible options.

not the Danes alone that unpack their hearts in words. We all do it. We are not mannequins you can measure, nor are we toys that utter prerecorded phrases. We are rational entities, and we seek to rationalize. We are living beings, generally mobile, and the purpose of our motion is not a subject of physics, but character.

Years ago, on one of the many history channels, I saw a run-of-the-mill documentary about Ancient Egypt. It was one of those shows that do not teach anything you do not already know, but, not attempting to present anything resembling entertainment, cannot fit any category except education. If my memory is correct, they talked about the nobility, and, as is common for history channels, they were showcasing a well-preserved mummy. The archaeologist (or journalist; whatever), a woman in her 30s or 40s, was fascinated by the corpse laid out in front of her. She looked at that former person's hands and remarked with something like reverence how we can still see the unique pattern on their fingertips. She went on gushing about the preservation. It never occurred to her that the fascinating thing about her subject was not ancient hierarchy, nor was it the fingerprints of the husk, but whatever had, at some point in the past, born those fingerprints as sign of touch – metaphorically, the deeds of that person, physically, the world they inhabited, and, humanely, the children those fingers might have held, or the parent that had once held them.

She was a scientist of the humanities (in as far as archaeology relates to history) but she spoke like a cold student of nature – making sure that the audience noticed the comfort she felt so close to the corpse, her indifference to its frozen snarl, and her fascination not with humanity, but with the skin on its shriveled fingers. The reader should remember the turncoats of two sections above: they wear the uniforms of humanists, but they really serve a foreign cause.

I will ask the reader to pardon me if in this third example I sound like Herodotus, but I must relay a story that, (I repeat, pardon my source) my cousin told me. She was a medical student on practice, and, one day, shortly after her tutelage began, as her mentor looked through the list of patients and their afflictions, she (the professor) kept musing to herself, *Now let's find us a nice heart attack – a really nice one, a pretty one*, and, upon finding a patient who had suffered heart trauma, she exclaimed, *Oh, there it is, this is a beautiful heart attack!*

My cousin, being a teenager at the time, and a white woman to this day, was as positively impressed at her professor's sociopathy no less than she gets giddy discussing serial killers. I suppose the lack of moral judgment on the part of my source suggests that it is at least somewhat trustworthy, seeing as she did not tell the story for the purpose of eliciting moral outrage.

All the same, I believe that the reader will begin to notice a pattern. Scientists, no matter their fields, in the role of prison guards, keep neglecting the human element in humanity, and make sure that others see them do it – they take pride in being disrespectful of the thing without which science would not be. They are happy to acknowledge the first clause as well as to ignore the second. It is not a secret lust either. On the contrary, it is overt and boisterous and impossible to ignore – and the more it shocks us, the better.

Perhaps the answer is becoming clearer now.

Why did the bully humiliate the nerd at recess?

It is no coincidence that it happened in public.

The Detective at Large

About a year ago, I had the good fortune of being introduced to a book I would not buy under normal circumstances. It was a collection of classic mysteries in the *flexibound* variety of which I have grown so fond, with a simple but unbelievably appealing cover, which corollary joke I will not make. Being a former Doyle purist, with an emphasis on *former* regarding my interest in the genre altogether, I did not originally intend to read it, however, it proved to be an instance where I am happy to have been wrong in my initial judgment. For those who are curious, I am talking about *Classic Tales of Mystery* by World Cloud Classics. With the exception of the last one, which was spy-fiction and therefore an intruder in the collection, I liked all of the stories: some I enjoyed a lot, and some of them I enjoyed for what they were.

Reading, I came across three stories that can serve to accentuate the purpose of this essay, which, I believe, should by a technique of broad strokes help to frame the conclusion to which I have been leading. These are *The Adventure of the Creeping Man*, by Sir Arthur Conan Doyle (1927), *The Blue Cross*, by G.K. Chesterton (1911), and *The Anthropologist at Large*, by R. Austin Freeman (1909). I believe a spoiler warning goes without saying. If any of these titles sounds interesting (the first two), I advise the reader to read them before continuing with this section.

The Adventure of the Creeping Man is a short story which has Holmes investigating the bizarre (seriously bizarre) behavior of a learned, well reputed man. It is important that this man is a respected member of society and that he is very intelligent. It is also important that he is an old man, and that he harbors a romantic interest for a young woman, who, though not entirely averse to his advances, would not commit herself to somebody his age. As Holmes spies on this gentleman, he sees him showing superb strength and agility. The man begins to harass his own dog, which eventually attacks him. The mystery is solved when Holmes discovers that the man had, in his possessions, serum that was supposed to make old men young again (at least in regards to virility), derived from the blood of langurs. It might feel like a cheap resolution (and it partly is) to evoke something as unnatural as that in generally grounded fiction, but one should note that overly potent serums at the time were not considered as silly as they are today. And like all good narrative that employs the common tropes of science fiction, it is in its non-fictional motifs that the breach of mundanity is justified. In the conclusion, Holmes notes that whenever a man tries to rise above nature, he is "liable to fall below it. The highest type of man may revert to the animal if he leaves the straight road of destiny." (Doyle). The contemporaneity of the plot should frame it as indirect criticism of the changing fashions at the time, in popular trend and in philosophy. That similar trends and philosophy still persist accounts for its timelessness. The story shows just how low a man can get attempting to pursue desires beyond what nature has destined for humanity, beginning with the humiliating act of one's (literal) apelike behavior, and ending with him being in mortal peril. It certainly is bizarre and weird and whatever else one might choose to call it, but the one thing it has going for it beyond debate is that it is perfectly human: this short story, simple though it is, reads like an ode to the holistic factuality of the human experience, specifically, at a time when humanity is becoming bored with itself. It talks of human yearnings such as love and eternal youth, it evokes human dread such as rejection and growing old, and it comments that, whatever alternative one may be offered, though it can, on occasion, diminish the cause of one's human fears, it will also diminish the correlation between one's identity and one's human nature. The dog attacking its progressively simian master was most likely written with the narrative purpose of suspense, though I will admit, it is tempting to note that it was nature's designated guardian that first detected the transgression against it.

The Blue Cross is a Father Brown story that follows a French detective as he pursues a French criminal across the gulf. Flambeau, the legendary thief, is after a precious blue cross that, at the time, is supposed to be in the hands of a diminutive Catholic priest who goes by the name Brown. The detective knows the whereabouts of neither. To wind up the suspense, he quickly learns that Brown's tactlessness had already attracted Flambeau, who is certain to steal the cross as soon as he gets the chance. As the detective tries to find them, he begins to catch note of peculiar events that constitute the talk of the day, all of which include two men of the clergy, and all of which constitute unusual behavior: a man paying for a window before he deliberately breaks it, fruit being rearranged in the market, soup thrown against a wall for no reason, and the salt and sugar having been swapped at a restaurant table. Following this trail of incidents, he eventually catches up to the two priests. They are in an isolated place, and he recognizes one of them as Father Brown. The other stands out with his impressive height. At this point, it is worth noting that Flambeau is supposed to be very tall. The detective (and the policemen he had called to his aid) move on to eavesdrop on their conversation. The story culminates with the twist that Brown knew all along that the man who pretended to be a student of divinity was in fact Flambeau. The incidents around town were caused by Brown himself, for they were meant to get them "talked about for the rest of the day" and to so attract the attention of the police (Chesterton, "Blue Cross"). Brown believed that a man who had nothing to hide would not keep quiet in a restaurant if there was salt in his coffee, or fail to react if his partner overpaid for a meal. That the tall cleric was content with drinking salted coffee as long as it meant keeping a low profile was evidence to Brown that his partner was likely an impostor. He began to suspect this, he said, because while discussing theology, Flambeau had tried to argue for a subjective view on reason. Philosophically, you can think whatever you want about theology, and, critically, you can argue what you will about the almost surreal amount of coincidences that need to have taken place for the story to unfold as it does. You may even call it a situational morality tale instead of proper detective fiction. But let us not let our literary pretenses obscure its brilliance: for all the criticism the critic might fling at it, *The Blue Cross* is a mystery with an effective twist, a wittily narrated plot, and valuable insights concerning the relations between secrecy and spontaneity, the mundane and the unusual, and reason and doctrine.

The Anthropologist at Large is the odd one out. Doctor Thorndyke is not quite a detective, but I shall opt to call him that for the sake of convenience (he does play the same part, after all). The brother of a wealthy man with an enormous art collection visits our protagonist with the kind of news you would expect him to bear: his brother's massive art collection had been robbed while he was away; it is unclear exactly what was stolen, since the art collection was too big to tell, and the only evidence left behind by the thief was his hat, which had been blown by the wind onto the neighbor's balcony. It was a cheap hat, and on it were traces of a particular dusty material. That suggested that it belonged to a factory worker. Studying the hat, the detective noticed that it belonged to a man with a small, round head. Inside, he found a sample of the thief's hair. The thickness of the individual piece of hair was thicker than that of white or black people. Thorndyke's inference was that it belonged to a poor Asian person, and, the detective argued, since the Japanese are physically the smallest of their race, his next objective was to track down Japanese factory workers. He was right. It was a Japanese man who stole Japanese art. The hair was thick, the man was small, and the dust was nacre. Case closed. There are no further points to be made about this story. It has no other motifs, it cannot boast of particularly witty writing, and it does not really inspire thought (other than *don't lose your hat when breaking the law!*). All it really does is confirm the deterministic fantasy of the natural sciences; the conformity of race, the brilliance of scientists, and the exactness of the material world in its inerrant glory.

The three stories speak of three very different protagonists: a borderline-sociopathic drug-abusing adventurer, an empathic and somewhat comical priest, and a natural scientist. But for all their differences, Holmes and Brown have something that Thorndyke does not: their stories are about humanity. They are about people with human desires making human decisions and human mistakes, and being caught by means of equally human processes. Brown exploits the spread of gossip, Holmes resorts to peering into a man's private life; Brown observes reactions, Holmes looks into patterns; Brown evaluates the way a man thinks, and Holmes comments on motives. They all deal with the unpredictable; with that which requires discussion and debate and, in spite of all logic, can lead to answers neither the reader nor the detectives expect. The competence of the investigators is to make sense of the mystery. The genius of the writers is to say as much as they can about as many things as the story allows. The appeal to the reader is that he wants to experience both deduction and contemplation. Freeman's story, on the other hand, is a one-sided excursus on nature. There is no emphasis on the human being; only an analysis of the human animal. There is no room for doubt – there are only three races, and only one of them matches the hair. The detective cannot go wrong, for he studies nature, and there is nothing wrong in nature. Stealing might be wrong, but the detective will not tell us why – his realm is not about what is either right or wrong (let alone why), but only that which is always right, namely the material world. The competence of the investigator is that he knows everything, the genius of the writer is that he made the investigator know everything, and the appeal to the reader is that he too can partake in the knowing of everything. There is no need for variables when the whole world can be rendered down to a constant. The anthropologist, you see, is not interested in humans – certainly not their minds or even the processes inside their brains. He is merely interested in their skulls.

Redefining the Final Frontier #.3

But let us ask ourselves: why were any of the examples in the second part even a thing? Why study infidelity, mummies, and fatal ailments? Why is infidelity such an emotional blow? Why is there a science about the forgotten lives of dead people? Why the fascination with that which kills?

We have already established that infidelity cannot be a problem of survival if we already have children (or if we do not care about children) or if a married bond ensures that one partner will not leave the other (or if the other partner is financially independent). Nor can it be the peculiarities of a specific culture that have made the issue so universal. Then again, is the word not hint enough on its own? Infidelity is not another word for sex. Infidelity is a synonym of treachery. It is not about Darwin, but Dante. Treachery is a moral crime that ruptures one's faith: in the other person, in oneself, and in the world as a whole – infidelity is only a specialized subset of the deed. I will here call attention to something in which all cases of betrayal are identical to infidelity, which is that there has never been a case in history where either betrayal or infidelity have been regarded as good things. Whereas some people in some contexts have argued that stealing, provided it is for a noble goal, can be noble, and even killing may be excused if it is in self-defense, there has never been a glorified traitor betraying gloriously or a noble cheater cheating nobly. Civilizations run on trust, and individuals are lost without it. The breach of trust is a problem of the spirit and a matter of the heart, and, between the two, it is an intrinsic element of human life.

One can hardly argue that the ancient Egyptians mummified their nobles because they wanted people thousands of years into the future to look upon them and say *Woah! Fingertips!* No. They did it to conserve life. They believed this would let them pass on into eternity. Like Socrates (Plato 608-9), they believed that life, by definition, must live on. They were human and they loved life, just as we are and just as we do, although we sometimes try to convince ourselves of the opposite.

The same applies to cardiology. Nobody would have studied it if not to preserve life, and nobody would have endeavored to preserve life if they did not love it. It is an inherently human thing: to study and to practice and to live so that others may live.

I have not read of other intelligent animals using and advancing and challenging their intelligence to help others of their specie (let alone different species) live on.

The answer is now visible and within reach.

Butch is picking on Marvin because Butch fears humanity. He fears life. Paradoxically, he fears death also. But at least he can pretend that he does not – and the dead will believe him. Dead things are simple things. They don't move. They don't change. They don't make you change. They cannot break your heart and they cannot make you feel stupid. The living, however, be it literal human beings or the metaphor of living ideas, just might call you out on your BS.

Deep down, we all fear the uncertainties of life. Up top, we try to suppress them with stories about constants, of a reality not only within reach but already in our grasp, clearly superior to the (so labeled) fantasies of the uneducated; so long as we do not have to experience the turbulent and the invisible and think to ourselves how lost we are, yet how much farther we must travel. It is best to write it off as an illusion, and then replace it with a factual illusion: we will count out the hours and we will call it a day.

The Theory in Practice

It is becoming clear that our culprit is indeed a relative of the Lernaean Hydra, that, having lost one head called Ignorance (no doubt to a thoughtless decision), has had its special power result in Stupidity and Cowardice. It is a terrifying beast indeed. One moment, you think you have triumphed over it, only to realize you have only made it stronger the next. It is foolish to hope for a better outcome. Intellect cannot arise from the carcass of its opposite. Dragon teeth need fertile soil to sprout. The ashes of the phoenix can only spawn birdbrains. But back to the Hydra and the metaphor of its polycephaly, I will now present a quick analysis of the two – of what stupidity and cowardice really mean, and, to the convinced, offer the chance to notice them in our present situation.

Ignorance, in as far as it signifies a lack of knowledge, is something of which we are all guilty, and, consequently, something of which none of us are guilty, for a vague *not knowing* is hardly a moral transgression. Ignorance is certainly not a good state in which to live, but in order for it to evolve into a problem, it must first be actualized as stupidity. Not to downplay the issue, I will warn you that it almost always does. Ignorance is like a tamed carnivore. As long as we keep paying attention, it could even make a cute pet. But, turn your back to it, and you can expect to feel its fangs in the nape of your neck. We do not call ignorance bliss just to deride the uneducated. There is a well of joy in precisely that which we do not know, and in all the time we have spent not studying it. Like petting a bear cub at the zoo, it may not be the best decision, but it is not always a horrible decision. It is only once we have let it have its way that it gets out of hand.

So it was never proof of stupidity that people (be it intelligent educated men or intelligent uneducated men or men who teach law) do not know history or that they do not care about philosophy or that culture has no place in their lexicon. The proof of stupidity is when this gap in knowledge allows for a kind of *wrong knowledge*, though an oxymoron, to enter where apprehension should have guarded against it. As soon as it has happened, it is no longer that one merely does not know, but that they *know* (or misknow) that it does not matter that one should know. This is a gateway to fallacy, logical and moral, and a wicked cycle of intellectual errors. It is like mixing sawdust with flour to make bread. By that I mean it is stupid.

A surefire way to recognize ignorance is to recognize contradiction. If a person can believe two things at the same time even though they cannot stand together, you can rest assured that they are indeed ignorant on at least one of them. Stupidity comes about when a person thinks that this is fine. They do not try to explain away the contradiction, which would be acceptable, or to even mask it as paradox, but instead assume that the contradiction must be true in spite of itself. Consider:

Numbers in isolation cannot determine meaning. Meaning is moot without numbers, including the meaning of numbers. Contemplation is part of non-material reality. There is only material reality, including our contemplation on material reality. Not all concepts can be accurately depicted as numbers. If a number will not suffice, then the relation between multiple numbers will. Two wrongs do not make a right. But three wrongs just might!

It is the conscious adherence to a contradictory frame of beliefs that qualifies an instance of stupidity. It could be a person who does not think for themselves and it could be a person who thinks too much of themselves. It could be a backwater rube and it could be an esteemed scholar (maybe even a scholar who takes monkey-serum). It could be somebody who clings to a religion that does not hold up, and it could be somebody who clings to a secularism that holds up but his self-image. Stupidity is not any belief in particular, but the evolution of a flawed belief into a feral, uncivilized, unstable kind of knowledge, which results in a degradation that makes man less manlike (akin to monkey-serum). It goes for the yokel and the Yale student alike: they have had their fun with their pet, and now they have turned their backs to it.

Cowardice is not as easy to define as one might think. On the one hand, it is a hyponym of submission. Both cover the same behavior, with cowardice relaying the more specific information: not all who submit are cowards, but all cowards submit. Cowardice is also a co-hyponym of irresponsibility, for it is the neglect of obligation in pursuit of comfort. So can we say then that a submissive person who is also irresponsible is a coward? Hardly. There are many irresponsible people that submit who do not fit the epithet. While we may be tempted to equate the concept with fear instead (or to succumbing to one's fear), the moral stipulation prohibits the possibility for such a general synonymy. Cowardice is inherently immoral. Fear is not. A man who runs from an escaped lion in the city zoo is certainly doing so in fear for his life; still, he cannot be called a coward, unless it was him that freed the lion from its confines. Nor is a man who runs from battle necessarily a coward; again, he did not necessarily ask that there should be war. But a man who begins a fight, drags his friends into it, and then runs away as soon as the fists start flying is surely deserving of the title.

But now that we have an example on which we can all agree, the definition of cowardice becomes slightly more accessible. The easiest would be to splice them all into one: an irresponsible person who, in submitting himself in fear, does an immoral act through his submission, is called a coward. There could be variations that might improve or diminish the accuracy of the wording, but let us try for something a bit more elegant. We may begin by asking – in what way does the immorality of the person who abandoned his friends present itself as a distinct kind of immorality? We could say *he started the fight and fled* and leave it at that, but this would not constitute cowardice if the people in question were not his friends – if he started a bar fight to defend himself, and the bar fight evolved into a mass fight between strangers, and so our subject fled the scene to avoid injury to his body; or if, though he started the fight, it was a fight between enemies. One would not call him a coward over that. Yet, imagine a person who got his friends into a fight and fled, only to later apologize and make up for his mistake – he tries his best at going above and beyond to atone for it. Though his initial act may have been cowardly, he is himself not a walking example of cowardice. That word would only apply if he does not try to make up for his mistake. If he first abandons his friends, and then keeps abandoning them by refusing to do what a friend ought to do. His motives also matter, and so does the camaraderie of his comrades. Having friends entails an obligation to these same friends: to do right by them and to help them and not mistreat them. It seems as though our exemplary coward is not quite known for running as much as betrayal. Do note, however, that while cowards are a treacherous lot indeed, the definition is not meant to take us a full circle back to infidelity.

A man who feels the urge to flee is a normal man. A man who flees is a scared man. And a man who flees his post is a deserter. But only a lying deserter is a coward. Now that we have begun to distinguish between manifestations, cowardice can begin to reveal its distinct meaning. Consider its co-hyponymy with irresponsibility, and consider the dependence of responsibility to the concept of consequence: there is no responsibility without the possibility of consequence, and there is no irresponsibility but the kind that risks it. This is the key to our definition. When a person steals, we merely call them a thief – they become a coward only when they run from the law. Nor do we call politicians cowards for refusing to take up arms and hit the trenches – we call them cowards for sending other men to war. Alternatively, we call politicians cowards when they run from the law after stealing. My point is that cowardice is the attempt to escape the consequences of one's actions – in particular, immoral actions. And there you have it, our working definition: cowardice is the perpetual avoidance of consequence. One desires something to further his own agenda; one does something, usually immoral, to get it; one fears the consequences that may arise from this, and so one does something even less morally sound to avoid them. He might prove a traitor, he might send a nation into disarray, he might jump into the lion's cage and sue the zoo, lie to his friends, or speak of democracy. Whatever he does, the one thing that is always on his mind is his own selfish desire, and the thing that determines his actions is his fear of what comes after.

So what do we say of men who wish to rule over the intellectual dimension of mankind, but, upon finding themselves neck-deep in self-contradiction, move on to bully their competition into obscurity? Men who would tell you that they are the only ones who get to make claims, then retreat to the position that they do not in fact make claims – they merely reject all your claims as patently meaningless? Men who hide behind numbers, men who put on masks of complexity, men who would mute that which they do not want to hear and have everybody listen to the one thing they do? I am rather fond of yellow, for I have too much debt to the sun to deride its robes as cowardly, but, for the sake of symbol, I believe these men would match the color.

The Final Frontier Redefined

It is funny. We have been trying to explain why volitional sociopaths have chosen to call our sense of empathy false. In short, the diagnostic portion of my essay could be summarized as a king who saw something scary, put out his eyes, and then outlawed painters.

So as we fear mental effort, so we accept scores in lieu of intelligence, because they make us feel superior without any labor. Though we fear moral interaction, we might yet profess moral relativism – it is the only scientifically viable morality after all, and by the only scientifically verifiable science. If we have succeeded at nothing significant, we could argue that *our bank accounts argue* that we have at least succeeded at something very big – *very big numbers*. Afraid of just how little we are worth, we decide that our net worth is more than a little. We cannot tell what makes a good man (or a good woman), but we just might be able to count their genetic traits as quality. The same goes for art. Besides, who is to say that fear of talent cannot be remedied by mathematical functions and talentless prompts? All the better if talent is left jobless in the process! Just as we dread the cost of improvement and instead speak of augmentations to give us improvement at no cost (upgrades and software and genetic alterations, all positive motifs in science-fiction; and plastic surgery and hormones, positive motifs in modern-day reality), so we preemptively lambast people who would cry *hard work and perseverance* lest we get caught speaking out against hard work and perseverance after the fact. What is man but a complex formula of atoms and delusions? What is left of man but a husk and fingertips? What is mankind but so much sentimental residue? Culture is effectively opium, history is historically politics, medicine was invented for cash; science is money, and economy proves it. Do you not see how proudly we proclaim it? That is intelligence, and we have the scores to confirm it! We have said a lot of meaningless things, only to conclude that meaninglessness is not so scary as long as we can count it.

So it was fear all along. Fear of ourselves and fear of who we were supposed to be – fear of just what we may discover if we dare venture in such topics. It was best to shut them off quickly. To liken them to the "Big Thinks" of Wells' character (Ch. 21): our human urges are the ramblings of a monkey-person. Surely, you would not want to be like that fictional monkey and think yourself man.

So cowardice and stupidity have ventured to intimidate us into remaining ignorant. And as like begets like, we have become stupid and cowardly in return. Ours was not a flattering fall. But the means of our liberation are corollaries to this fact. If our incarceration began as cowardice, then our freedom must begin with valor. Intellectual valor, above all, but also valor of purpose and of emotion, which, far from mindlessness, must be the mature emotion of adults. In times like these, it is comforting to know that courage is "being scared to death, but saddling up anyway" (Morrison).

Beyond the Walls

If the prison is circular, as is the fallacy that built it, then the prison is also ignorance, for fallacy is just a facet of intellectual deprivation. I do not say this to offend. I merely note the lack of intellectual input. Of course, mind is the only non-destructive counter to ignorance. That is the good news, and the reason I bring it up. The other headline, however, is that the tool we have lost is none other than the tradition of mind. We have gone a long way to rust the only thing standing between us and the tyranny of King Ignoramus. Fortunately, and possibly even providentially, it can be retrieved once we know where to look.

The metaphor with child neglect still stands. Their forgotten names are crucial to the conceptual frame of the prison. So all we need to do for a start is to call out to them. Let us begin with the basics: good, evil, wisdom, insanity, humanity... these should be intuitive – like riding a bike, one cannot completely forget them. As soon as we have appealed to them, the ideas will come back to us running. They will visit us outside the prison walls, on the other side of the fence and just past the windows, they will answer and they will talk to us. We may then proceed to converse to one another about them. As we begin remembering, memories will keep returning. Soon, we will call out to more nuanced ideas: manhood and womanhood, language, intelligence, success, art, respect.[24] Courage will have strengthened our minds, and our minds will proceed to weaken the wardens. The gates will begin to creak, and the guards will grow less powerful by the thought.

In the least optimistic scenario, though we will not leave the prison in body, we will do so in speech... just as we have remembered the names of our children, they will remember our names, and we will live on beyond the walls; maybe not in person, but definitely in name. We will have joined that great lineage of mental tradition that has brought us up, and, once stupidly lost, we have managed to courageously retrieve. It is a hero's fate.

But there is a more optimistic alternative. It is the conversion of the prison. The more we talk to one another, the wiser we

---

[24] I will cover these in the essays that follow.

become. The more people awaken, the more our community will grow. The grounds of our current enslavement will begin to resemble autonomous territory. The guards may try to stop us, but they are powerless if we do not engage them. They hold power over puppets, not men. There is no reason to fight them. Remember that they do not even have the key, for they are also shackled in ignorance. So until the gates open, we will do the next best thing: we will turn Pythagoras' prison into Pythagoras' forum. The prison yard will be converted into a hub of freedom, cells will turn into offices, and the institution (or part of it) will have become a university. We will not work to get out of the prison, but to get the warden out of us. And we just might find the gates have molten down in the meantime.

<u>Another Word</u>

I am (predominantly) a fiction writer. It is telling when the metaphor I have applied to an issue in the modern zeitgeist has grown into a shape that could work just as well (and arguably better) in a different medium; perhaps a surrealist short story. And it has grown indeed: beginning with a bizarre lapse in mental acuity wherewith mankind has lost all memory of its ancestors; followed by criminal neglect, fraudulent doctors, and puppet-masters-turned-prison-wardens to outplay the legal system. Then followed the twist that all of us play the wardens from time to time, and the revelation that the way out is not escape, but conversion of the territory. After all, it was quite the concept that the villain stares back at us from a dismorphic mirror: he is insecurity incarnate. And now, we shall proceed to fight him back with the help of feral children carrying the voice of our ancestors! It sounds epic, put in those words, though in the material world it is a feat no more impressive than sitting broodingly in an armchair, and so only for those rich enough to afford one.

Sometimes, one writes fiction and discovers philosophy. Today, I have completed an attempt at (casual) philosophy and got an idea for a piece of fiction – the script for a short animated film, to be exact, which I intend to make.

But now that we are back in reality, I would like to thank you for reading so far. I have written a much longer text than I had expected. I was aiming for ten to fifteen pages. The metaphor has taken us all over the conceptual spectrum, though I'd be lying if I said I would have it any other way.

And as I struggle to think of a conclusion, I can only comment that a conclusion does not make much sense in an introductory essay. This is only the beginning. But it should make sense in a text that nevertheless claims to stand on its own.

So I will call back to the initial step for breaking our intellectual confinement: courage. It just might offer a brief answer to the subtitle with which I began my essay: _What is a man?_

Heroism differs from other forms of sacrifice (even volitional forms) in the sense that a hero has no guarantee of success: heroism is a choice made in good faith, and with the conviction not that the heroic sacrifice will bring about a heroic result, but that the sacrifice made is the only right choice: the only way to tell the enemy to stuff it, and the only way to prove to oneself that one has _what it takes_ to call oneself free – product be damned; and as heroes die, it is their character that lives on, that we celebrate annually, and that we think about whenever that same duty falls upon ourselves – do we continue as happy slaves, or do we take up the mantle, and ride on to the test of valor?

I hope to see you all at the forum.

END of PART 1

<u>References and such – for those who really *really* care...</u>

Chesterton, Gilbert K.
---. "The Blue Cross." *The Innocence of Father Brown*, 1911.
---. "The Fallacy of Success." *All Things Considered*, 1915.

Doyle, Arthur C. "The Adventure of the Creeping Man." *The Case-Book of Sherlock Holmes*, 1927. Project Gutenberg, 2023.

Freeman, Richard A. "The Anthropologist at Large." *John Thorndyke's Cases*, 1909. Internet Archive: Digital Library, 2017.

Morrison, Marion R. [people online agree that he most certainly said it, though the source of when and where he said it seems to be our collective unconscious].

Plato. "Phaedo." *Great Dialogues of Plato*, translated by William Henry Denham, edited by Eric H. Warmington. Rouse, Signet Classics, 2015.

Sayers, Dorothy. *Whose Body?*. 1923. Project Gutenberg, 2019.

Wells, Herbert G. *The Island of Doctor Morreau*. 1896. Project Gutenberg, 2004.

World Cloud Classics. *Classic Tales of Mystery*. Canterbury Classics, 2020.

<u>In this Series...</u>

<u>*Pythagoras' Prison*</u>

In this introductory essay, the author explains the structure of our conceptual prison, the danger of its illusion, and the circumstances surrounding its creation – ideological, practical, and personal.

Through an elaborate metaphor of crime, toymakers, and an asylum, Pythagoras' Prison is written to illustrate the modern fallacy and to refocus the purpose of thought onto its original trajectory.

<u>*An Essay Concerning Human Misunderstanding*</u>

An Essay Concerning Human Misunderstanding is the central entry in the eponymous series. It is a meditation on a selection of contemporary passions that burden the modern citizen. Relying on linguistic science, philosophical appeal, and human curiosity, it locates their origin in a conceptual error, which discovery is at once to the reader's satisfaction and the means of recovery.

<u>*Bards, Robots, and Hordes*</u>

A treatise on defeat as an outcome not at all humiliating: sometimes, it is not triumph that determiners winner from loser. There follow three essays: on art; artificial intelligence; and mankind's regression into the primitive commune known as a horde – an uncaring, uneducated, and untrusting population. It is about deception by ornament, an unusual orphanhood, and conceptual deterioration... a conclusion just shy of optimistic goes without saying.

<u>Also by Hank Youngman...</u>

<u>*The Chapbooks Trilogy*</u>

A printed collection of 50 poems and 3 essays, divided in three parts according to form and subject matter: *Ambition in Vain*, *Songlets*, and *Chapbook #3*.
Each part can also be purchased independently as a digital copy.

<u>*It Comes with the Territory*</u>

A science-fiction mystery adventure with an emphasis on the real-world factors that enable the grounds for the plot. Written in the tradition of classic science fiction, *It Comes with the Territory* aims to entertain, in as far as the reader enjoys mystery adventures, as well as to inspire thought, in as far as the reader is accustomed to thinking.

<u>*The Playwright*</u>

Set in a plot that is in the same measure natural and supernatural, *The Playwright* is a unique take on the ghost story as narrated in a modern context – a work of mystery, suspense, and light horror, it is an ideal read for the modern enthusiast of the genre.

<u>*A Righteous Agenda*</u>

A work of mystery, suspense, and light satire that aims to provide an intriguing set of characters and events, with a twist that is subtly foretold yet remains just out of grasp until the conclusion.